Chinese Recipes

TARLA DALAL
India's # 1 Cookery Author

S&C
SANJAY & CO.
MUMBAI

Second Printing : 2007

ISBN : 978-8-189491-23-9

Price: Rs. 89/-

Published & Distributed by : **Sanjay & Company**

353/A-1, Shah & Nahar Industrial Estate, Dhanraj Mill Compound, Lower Parel (W), Mumbai - 400 013. INDIA.

Tel. : (91-22) 2496 8068 • Fax : (91-22) 2496 5876 • E-mail : sanjay@tarladalal.com

Recipe Research & Production Design
Arati Fedane
Umaima Abdulally

Nutritionist
Nisha Katira
Sapna Kamdar

Food Styling
Shubhangi Dhaimade

Photography
Jignesh Jhaveri

Typesetting
Adityas Enterprises

Designed by
Satyamangal Rege

Printed by :
Minal Sales Agencies, Mumbai

DISCLAIMER

While every precaution has been taken in the preparation of this book, the publishers and the author assume no responsibility for errors or omissions. Neither is any liability assumed for damages resulting from the use of information contained herein. And of course, no book is a substitute for a qualified medical advice. So it is wiser to modify your dietary patterns under the supervision of a doctor or a nutritionist.

INTRODUCTION

Dear Friends,

The trend is in favour of Chinese food. People have begun to enjoy the versatile cuisine of China, making it extremely popular world over.

While assembling and preparing the ingredients is a laborious task, the actual cooking of Chinese food takes barely a few minutes. This ensures that the food is cooked to perfection, retaining the fresh flavour and distinct texture of each of the many ingredients. It's the cheery taste and crispiness of food that sets Chinese cuisine a class apart.

Like India, China is a vast country with pronounced differences in regional cuisines. Chinese cuisine can be broadly classified based on region into Peking, Tianjin, Shanghai and Guangzhou (Canton). I have discovered that the Cantonese and Schezuan styles of cooking appeal to the Indian palate more than their blander counterparts. In India, like elsewhere in the world, we have adapted Chinese food to suit local tastes. Here we are partial to stronger spices and sauces. The food in China might not taste anything like the modified versions that you relish in Chinese restaurants closer home!

However, I have tried to ensure that the recipes of popular Cantonese and Schezuan dishes included in this book, such as the **Hakka Noodles, Vegetable Wontons, Triple**

Schezuan Rice, Sweet and Sour Vegetables and Khimchi, are all as authentic as possible. To make things simpler for you I have avoided exotic ingredients that are not easily accessible across India. All the ingredients featured in these recipes can be found in most provision stores and supermarkets. Even the novice cook will find these recipes easy to follow, and will enjoy the amazing results.

Set up your own Chinese kitchen at home, experiment and innovate with the ingredients and exotic sauces, and enjoy a healthy and immensely satisfying Oriental eating experience within the privacy and warmth of your own home, whenever you want!

Regards,

Tarla Dalal

CONTENTS

RICE

VEGETABLE DISHES

ACCOMPANIMENTS

BASIC RECIPES

CHINESE COOKING BASICS

To make your Chinese dishes as authentic and delicious as possible, it is vital that you prepare the ingredients correctly. Illustrated below are a few simple ways to prepare all your ingredients the perfect way...

Cutting

It is important to remember that cutting before cooking introduces harmony and brings out the true flavours of the ingredients. Thinly cut ingredients cook very quickly and the short cooking time ensures that the natural flavours are preserved.

The food should be cut into units of roughly the *same shape, size and thickness*. If the main ingredient of a recipe is shredded, then so are the other ingredients. Use a sharp knife or invest in a Chinese cleaver for best results.

The four basic cutting methods are as follows:

***Slicing*:** Here, the ingredients are cut into thin slices, about the size of a postage stamp, but as thin as cardboard.

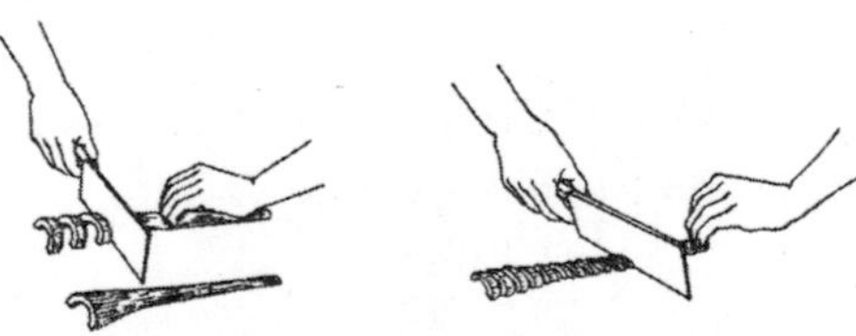

***Diagonal cutting*:** This method is normally used for cutting vegetables such as carrots, celery or courgettes. Roll the vegetables half a turn each time you make a diagonal cut straight down.

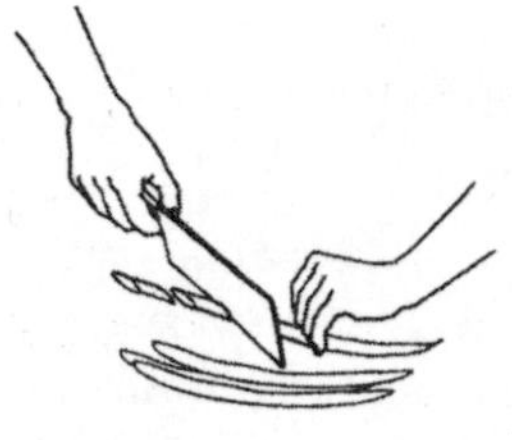

***Shredding/Cutting in to thin strips*:** While shredding, the ingredients are first cut into thin slices, stacked like a pack of playing cards, and then cut into thin strips.

Cubes: The ingredients are first cut into strips as wide as they are thick, then the strips are cut at right angles in the same width so they become small squares.

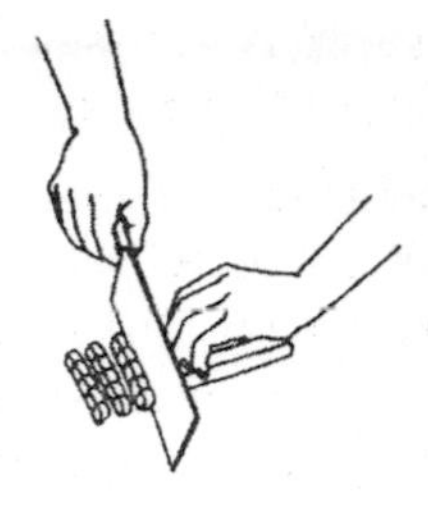

Stir-Frying

While the Chinese use various cooking methods, their unique contribution to the culinary art is Stir-Frying. A Chinese immigrant to the United States described the process as, "a big fire - shallow fat - continuous stirring - quick frying of cut up ingredients with wet seasoning." Funny as it may sound, stir-frying is just that!

Stir-frying is a great way to quickly put together a main dish that's low in fat and high in nutrition. It takes advantage of a new approach to eating that helps protect against chronic diseases. Prepared properly, a stir-fry is low in calories and fat.

The food to be cooked is first cut into uniform bite-sized pieces. This ensures that the maximum surface area is exposed to heat while stir-frying, thus cooking the food quickly and evenly.

How to stir-fry?

Heat oil in a pre-heated wok over high heat, then throw in the ingredients and constantly stir and toss them for a short while. Timing is of utmost importance as over-cooking will turn the food into a soggy mess. When correctly done, the *food will be crispy and wholesome*.

While stir-frying, very little or no water is added, since the high heat will bring out the natural juices from the fresh ingredients. For best results, use good quality ingredients that are fresh. In fact, in Chinese cooking, the quality of the final product depends entirely on the quality of raw ingredients used. Since most of the stir-fried recipes make sparse use of seasoning and flavouring agents, the flavours of the staple ingredients dominate the dish.

One must be able to control the heat with perfect ease, as it is vital to turn it down or bring it up at crucial moments during the cooking process. If the heat is too high for too long the food may end up either over-cooked or unevenly cooked, that is, burnt outside and raw inside. With a little bit of practice, you will get the hang of when to adjust the heat during the cooking process.

Another notable aspect of stir-frying is the pan in which it is actually done. The WOK, as the pan is called, is a magic vessel! It is interesting to note that the entire spectrum of Chinese cooking methods can be executed in that one single utensil itself.

CHINESE UTENSILS

The basic Chinese utensils the wok and the cleaver, which the Chinese chefs use with great skill and dexterity are exemplary of traditional Chinese ingenuity.

The Wok

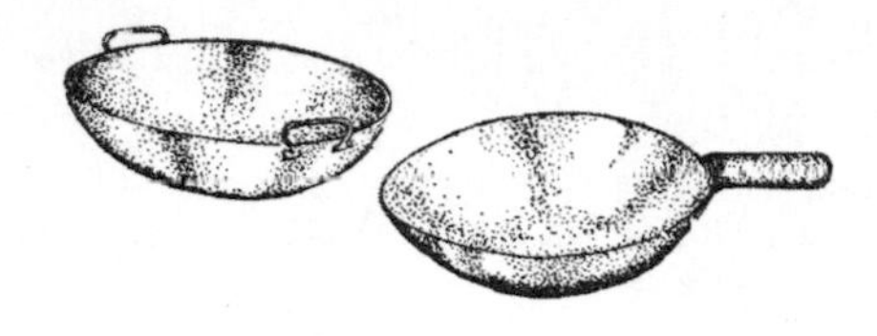

The wok is a superb, versatile vessel which can be used to execute most Chinese cooking methods.

The Chinese Cleaver (Chopper)

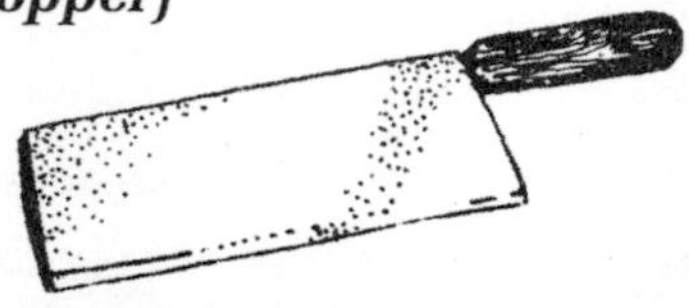

The cleaver is as magical as the wok and makes itself useful as a one-stop solution for almost all chopping and pounding tasks.

How to use the cleaver

The lighter front half of the blade is used for slicing, shredding, scoring etc and the heavier rear half of the blade is for chopping and so on. You can use the back of the blade for pounding and tenderizing and the flat side of the blade for crushing and transporting. The end of the handle can even be used as a pestle for grinding spices etc.

GLOSSARY

Some of the ingredients used in this book may be quite a mystery to many of you. I remember how baffled I was with some of them when I started experimenting with Chinese cooking. So, in order to clarify common doubts, we have listed and explained a few of the ingredients used in this book.

Chinese 5 Spice Powder

5 Spice Powder is a powdered mixture of fennel seeds (*saunf*), cloves (*laung / lavang*), cinnamon (*dalchini*), star anise (*dagad phool*), schezuan peppers in the ratio 1 : ½ : 1 : 2 : 2. It is slightly sweet and pungent and has to be stored tightly covered, in a dry place at room temperature.

Hoisin Sauce

Hoisin sauce, which is widely used in Chinese cooking, is thick, reddish-brown in colour, sweet and spicy. This mixture of soybeans, garlic, pepper and various other spices is easily available at leading provision stores. Once opened, canned *hoisin* should be transferred to a non-metal container, tightly sealed and refrigerated. Bottled *hoisin* sauce can be refrigerated as it is. Both will keep indefinitely when stored in this manner.

MSG (Mono Sodium Glutamate)

Commonly referred to in India as Ajinomoto, MSG is a flavouring agent used extensively in Chinese cuisine. A Japanese firm first sold it under the name Ajinomoto meaning "prime element of taste" and since then Mono Sodium Glutamate has been synonymous with the name Ajinomoto.

MSG helps enhance the taste of food and is made mostly from the gluten of flour. Recently there have been many controversies regarding its usage. I would recommend that children and pregnant women avoid consuming it even at restaurants.

I have omitted it in many of these recipes and have added it only as an option, in some recipes.

Rice Noodles

These extremely thin Chinese noodles resemble long, translucent white hair. When deep-fried, they explode dramatically into a tangle of airy, crunchy strands that are used for garnishing. Rice noodles are also used in soups and stir-fries. They are usually sold as coiled nests packaged in cellophane paper, and are easily available at most provision stores.

Tofu (Soya *paneer*)

Tofu is made from soya bean milk and has a very distinct flavour and smell. It is easily perishable and should be kept submerged in water in the refrigerator. It can be kept for a couple of days if the water is changed daily.

Locally known as Soya Paneer, it is easily available in most large grocery stores and health food stores. One can safely use paneer (cottage cheese) as a substitute for tofu.

Vegetable Stock

Vegetable stock is an important flavouring agent for most Chinese soups and gravies. In the traditional Chinese kitchen, a pot of hot liquid with all vegetable scraps is always kept ready for use. The stock gives body to the soups and gravies. However, if you do not have any stock at hand and if you feel too lazy to make some, then you could substitute it with seasoning cubes mixed in water.

Vegetarian Oyster Sauce

A dark-brown sauce consisting of vegetable extracts, brine and soy sauce cooked until thick and concentrated. Oyster sauce imparts richness to dishes without overpowering their natural flavour. It is available at most leading provision stores.

Wonton/Spring Roll Wrappers

These thin, soft squares of dough are made with plain flour (*maida*) and water. They are filled with vegetable mixtures and then deep-fried or steamed. They are sold, either frozen or refrigerated, at most leading provision stores. *Samosa Paṭtis* can be used as a substitute for wonton wrappers.

Crispy Threaded Tofu

Picture on page 19.

Good to see, good to eat, this starter looks like a cute little bird's nest.

Preparation time: 10 minutes. Cooking time: 5 minutes. Makes 15.

15 (1″) cubes of tofu (soya *paneer)*
15 wonton/spring roll wrappers
½ cup Schezuan sauce, page 91
1 tbsp cornflour
Salt to taste

How to proceed

1. Make a marinade using Schezuan sauce, cornflour, salt and 2 tbsp of water.
2. Marinate the tofu cubes in it for 5 to 10 minutes. Keep aside.

3. Place a wrapper on a plain surface and make small slits at equal distance on one horizontal top side with a sharp knife. Repeat with the remaining 14 wrappers and keep aside.
4. Take a cube of marinated tofu and place it on one end of the wrapper. Apply the marinade along the edges and bring the ends together to form a crown like fringe at one side as shown in the picture on facing page. Press so the end sticks.
5. Deep-fry the wrappers in hot oil till golden brown and crisp.
6. Repeat with the remaining 14 wrappers and tofu cubes.

   Serve hot with a sauce of your choice.

VARIATION: You can use paneer instead of tofu for a variation of the recipe.

CRISPY THREADED TOFU : Recipe on page 17. →

Spring Rolls

These tasty spring rolls are jam-packed with the goodness of vegetables. Remember to drain the filling thoroughly in order to ensure a dry, cohesive mixture. Also make sure you seal the rolls securely so they don't break open while frying.

Preparation time: 15 minutes. Cooking time: 30 minutes. Makes 12 rolls.

12 readymade spring roll wrappers
3 tbsp plain flour *(maida)* mixed with ¼ cup of water
Oil for deep-frying

For the stuffing
½ cup chopped spring onion whites
1½ cups mixed vegetables (French beans, carrots and cabbage), cut into thin strips
¾ cup bean sprouts
¾ tsp MSG (Mono Sodium Glutamate), optional
½ cup boiled hakka noodles, cut into 1″ pieces, page 99
2 tsp soya sauce
½ cup chopped spring onion greens
1 tbsp oil

Salt to taste

To serve
Chilli garlic sauce, page 93

For the stuffing

1. Heat the oil in a wok over a high flame. Add the spring onion whites, mixed vegetables, bean sprouts and MSG and stir-fry for 3 to 4 minutes.
2. Add the noodles, soya sauce and salt and cook for 2 more minutes. Cool and keep aside.
3. Switch off the flame, add the spring onion greens and mix well.

How to proceed

1. Place one spring roll wrapper on a dry surface and spoon a little of the stuffing mixture on one end of the wrapper.
2. Roll the spring roll wrapper tightly, sealing the ends securely with the flour paste.
3. Repeat with the remaining ingredients to make 11 more spring rolls.
4. Deep fry in hot oil till they are golden brown. Drain on absorbent paper.
5. Cut each roll at an angle into two and serve hot.

Handy Tip: The easiest way to cut boiled noodles is to put them in a bowl and use scissors to cut them.

VARIATION : **VEGETABLE WONTONS**

Use the same wrapper but cut into circles of about 40 mm. diameter, put a little stuffing in the centre, fold over to make a semi-circle. Then bring the ends together and press so they stick. Deep-fry till golden brown or steam in a greased steamer for 12-15 minutes. Serve hot.

Vegetable Dumplings

Vegetable dumplings are popularly called dimsums. To making perfect dumplings, ensure that the outer covering is rolled very thinly.

Preparation time: 15 minutes. Cooking time: 30 minutes. Makes 25 rolls.

For the dough
2 cups plain flour *(maida)*
2 tbsp oil
Salt to taste

For the vegetable filling
1 cup shredded cabbage
1 cup shredded carrot
½ cup chopped mushrooms
½ cup chopped asparagus
1 tbsp chopped ginger
1 tsp pepper powder
6 tbsp soya sauce
Salt to taste

For the red sauce
2 tomatoes
6 cloves garlic
4 whole dry red chillies
Salt to taste

For the black sauce
¼ cup soya sauce
1 tbsp honey
2 tsp vinegar
2 tsp roasted sesame seeds *(til)*
Salt to taste

Other ingredients
Oil for greasing

For the dough
1. Combine all the ingredients and knead into a soft pliable dough.
2. Roll out into a big cylinder.
3. Divide the dough into small 25 equal portions. Keep aside.

For the vegetable filling

1. Heat the oil in the wok over a high flame, add the ginger and sauté for a few seconds.
2. Add all the remaining ingredients and stir-fry for a couple of minutes.
3. Remove from heat and divide into 25 equal portions. Keep aside to cool.

For the red sauce

1. Put the tomatoes in a vesselful of boiling water for 2-3 minutes. Remove peel and chop roughly and peel the tomatoes. Keep aside.
2. Dry roast the red chillies till they are crisp. Keep aside.
3. Combine the tomatoes, garlic, red chillies and salt and blend to a smooth purée in a blender. Keep aside.

For the black sauce

Combine all the ingredients and mix well. Keep aside.

How to proceed

1. Roll out each portion of the dough into very thin circles of approximately 75 mm. (3") diameter.
2. Place one portion of the vegetable filling in the centre of each circle.
3. Bring together the edges and with your fingertips to make dimsums.
4. Steam in a greased steamer for about 10 minutes.
   Serve hot with the red and black sauces.

Baby Corn Salt and Pepper

Quick and easy to make, this stir-fry tingles the taste buds.

Preparation time: 15 minutes. Cooking time: 15 minutes. Serves 4.

3 cups blanched baby corn, cut into 1" pieces
¼ cup cornflour
¾ cup sliced whole spring onions
1 tbsp finely chopped garlic
1 tbsp whole peppercorns
1 tbsp oil
Salt to taste
Oil for frying

1. Dry roast the peppercorns in a wok over a medium flame for a few minutes, grind coarsely and keep aside.
2. Mix together the cornflour, salt, 1 tsp of coarsely ground pepper and ¼ cup of cold water.
3. Dip the baby corn in this mixture and deep-fry till golden brown. Drain on absorbent paper and keep aside
4. Heat the oil in a wok, over a high flame, add the spring onions, garlic, the remaining pepper and salt and stir-fry for 1 minute.
5. Add the fried baby corn and toss well. Serve hot.

Crispy Lotus Stem Honey Chilli

Picture on page 1.

Though traditionally associated with Sindhi cuisine, it looks like lotus stem can be made into a great Chinese starter too!

Preparation time: 15 minutes. Cooking time: 10 minutes. Serves 4.

2 cups thinly sliced lotus stem *(bhein)*, washed well
¼ cup cornflour
⅓ cup honey
1 tbsp dry red chillli flakes
⅓ cup tomato ketchup
2 tbsp soya sauce
2 tbsp chilli oil, page 102
Salt to taste
Oil for deep-frying

1. Dust the lotus stem slices with cornflour and deep-fry in hot oil until crisp. Drain on absorbent paper and keep aside.
2. Heat the oil in the wok over a high flame and add the remaining ingredients.
3. Add the fried lotus stem slices.
4. Toss well until the sauce coats the lotus stems and serve hot.

Handy tip : Ensure that the lotus stems are cleaned thoroughly before you slice them.

Pearly Corn

These yummy corn tit-bits look like small pearls when fried; no wonder it's called pearly corn.

Preparation time: 10 minutes. Cooking time: 15 minutes. Serves 4.

1 cup sweet corn kernels (*makai ke dane*)
½ cup plain flour *(maida)*
¼ cup cornflour
½ tsp readymade mustard paste
1 tsp chilli powder
½ cup water
Salt and pepper to taste
Oil for deep-frying

For the garnish
2 tbsp chopped spring onion greens

1. Mix together all the ingredients except the oil in a bowl and keep aside.
2. Heat the oil in a wok, over a high flame and scatter individual batter coated kernels in the oil. Deep-fry until they are golden brown in colour and drain on absorbent paper. Serve immediately, garnished with the spring onion greens.

Sweet Corn Soup

The delicate and pleasant flavour of corn makes this a popular choice. Enjoy it sweet and simple or spike with chillies in vinegar.

Preparation time: 10 minutes. Cooking time: 20 minutes. Serves 4.

½ cup crushed sweet corn kernels (*makai ke dane*)
¾ cup grated sweet corn kernels (*makai ke dane*)
4 cups clear vegetable stock, page 97
3 tbsp cornflour mixed with ¼ cup water
1 tsp sugar, optional
Salt to taste

To serve
Chillies in vinegar, page 90
Soya sauce
Chilli sauce

1. Put the stock in a pan and add the crushed sweet corn kernels.
2. Cover and cook over a medium flame for approx. 10 minutes or till the corn is tender.
3. Add the cornflour paste and simmer for some time.
4. Add the grated sweet corn kernels and simmer for another 5 minutes.
5. Add the sugar and salt and serve hot with chillies in vinegar, soya sauce and chilli sauce.

Handy tip: For a quicker version, just mix some water and cornflour mixture in a can of cream style corn and bring to a boil.

Manchow Soup

An all-time favourite, this soup is an ideal starter for any meal. The sharp flavours of ginger and garlic merge beautifully with the fresh flavour of herbs like coriander and mint, in this soya sauce based soup.

Preparation time: 15 minutes. Cooking time: 10 minutes. Serves 4.

2 tbsp finely chopped tomatoes
2 tbsp finely chopped cauliflower
2 tbsp finely chopped carrots
2 tbsp finely chopped cabbage
2 tsp finely chopped garlic
2 tsp chopped ginger
4½ cups clear vegetable stock , page 97
1 tbsp finely chopped fresh mint leaves (*phudina*)
1 tbsp chopped coriander
3 tsp soya sauce
2 tbsp cornflour dissolved in ½ cup water
A pinch MSG (Mono Sodium Glutamate), optional

1 tbsp oil
Salt and pepper to taste

For the topping
Chilli oil, page 102
Chopped coriander

1. Heat the oil in a wok over a high flame. Add the garlic, ginger, tomatoes, cauliflower, carrot, cabbage and MSG and stir-fry for 2 to 3 minutes.
2. Add the stock, mint, coriander, soya sauce, salt and pepper.
3. Add the cornflour mixture to the soup and boil for 1 minute. Top with the chilli oil and coriander.
   Serve hot.

Bean Sprouts Soup

It cooks amazingly fast and has a simple, yet tantalizing flavour.

Preparation time: 2 minutes. Cooking time: 5 minutes. Makes 4 cups.

½ cup finely chopped spring onion whites
¼ cup finely chopped red capsicum
¼ cup finely chopped green capsicum
¾ cup bean sprouts
2 tsp soya sauce
2 tbsp oil
Salt and pepper to taste

To serve
Soya sauce
Chillies in vinegar, page 90

1. Boil 3 cups of water. Keep aside.
2. Heat the oil in a wok over a high flame, add the spring onions whites, red capsicum and green capsicum and stir-fry for 2 minutes.
3. Add the bean sprouts and stir-fry for another minute.
4. Add the boiling water, salt and pepper and bring to boil.
5. Add the soya sauce and mix well.
   Serve hot with soya sauce and chillies in vinegar.

Hot and Sour Soup

Picture on page 37.

A wonderful blend of hot and sour flavours, this is the perfect choice for a lazy winter evening.

Preparation time: 20 minutes. Cooking time: 5 minutes. Serves 4.

½ cup shredded cabbage
½ cup grated carrots
½ cup finely chopped cauliflower
¼ cup chopped spring onions
2 pinches MSG (Mono Sodium Glutamate), optional
3½ cups clear vegetable stock, page 97
2 tbsp vinegar
1 tbsp soya sauce
½ tsp chilli sauce
1 tbsp chopped coriander
3 tbsp cornflour dissolved in ½ cup water
2 tbsp oil

Salt and freshly ground pepper to taste

For the garnish
1 tbsp chopped coriander

1. Heat the oil in a wok over a high flame. Add the cabbage, carrots, cauliflower, spring onions and MSG and stir-fry over a high flame for 2 minutes.
2. Add the stock, vinegar, soya sauce, chilli sauce, coriander, pepper and salt and simmer for 2 minutes.
3. Add the cornflour mixture and boil for 3 to 4 minutes while stirring continuously. Serve hot garnished with coriander.

HOT AND SOUR SOUP : Recipe on page 35. →

Talumein Soup

Picture on back cover.

Relax with a cup of Talumein soup and revel in its amazingly balanced flavours.

Preparation time: 10 minutes. Cooking time: 10 minutes. Serves 6.

1 cup finely chopped mixed vegetables (carrots, cabbage, spring onions, cauliflower)
A pinch of MSG (Mono Sodium Glutamate), optional
½ cup grated corn (makai ke dane)
4 cups clear vegetable stock, page 97
½ tsp soya sauce
½ tsp sugar
¾ cup raw hakka noodles, broken into 50 mm. (2″) length
3 tbsp corn flour dissolved in ¾ cup of water
2 tbsp oil
Salt and pepper to taste

For the garnish
2 tbsp finely chopped spring onions
1 tbsp finely chopped coriander

To serve
Chillies in vinegar, page 90
Chilli sauce
Chilli oil, page 102

1. Heat the oil in a wok over a high flame, add the mixed vegetables and MSG and stir-fry for a couple of minutes.
2. Add the corn, vegetable stock, soya sauce, sugar, noodles, salt and pepper and bring to boil.
3. Add the corn flour mixture and stir continuously till the soup thickens.
4. Garnish with the chopped spring onions and coriander.
   Serve hot with chillies in vinegar, chilli sauce and chilli oil.

Crispy Rice and Noodle Soup

Crispy, crackling rice when added to this soup, serves as a sizzling start to your meal.

Preparation time: 10 minutes. Cooking time: 10 minutes. Serves 4.

½ cup boiled hakka noodles, cut into 2" pieces
½ cup finely chopped cauliflower
¼ cup sliced carrots
1 tbsp chopped celery
2 tbsp chopped spring onion whites
¼ tsp MSG (Mono Sodium Glutamate), optional
¼ cup tomatoes, cut into small pieces
2 tbsp chopped lettuce leaves
4 cups clear vegetable stock, page 97
2 tbsp oil
Salt to taste

For the garnish
2 tbsp crispy rice, page 101

2 tbsp crispy fried noodles, page 100

To serve
Chillies in vinegar, page 90
Chilli sauce

1. Heat the oil in a wok over a high flame, add the cauliflower, carrots, celery, spring onion whites and MSG and sauté for 3 to 4 minutes.
2. Heat the stock, add the sauté
   ed vegetables, tomato pieces, lettuce and salt and allow it to come to a boil. Add the noodles and switch off the flame.
3. Pour into a large serving bowl.
4. Just before serving, sprinkle the crispy rice and fried noodles over the soup and serve immediately with chillies in vinegar and chilli sauce.

Handy Tip: The easiest way to cut boiled noodles is to put them in a bowl and use scissors to cut them.

Noodles

Hakka Noodles

A simple dish of noodles tossed with garlic, vegetables and any other ingredients of your choice, like mushrooms etc., this all-time favourite gets its name from the Chinese province of Hakka.

Preparation time: 10 minutes. Cooking time: 10 minutes. Serves 4.

4 cups boiled hakka noodles, page 99
3 tsp chopped garlic
3 whole dry red chillies, broken into pieces
1½ cups shredded cabbage
1 cup finely sliced capsicum
½ cup chopped spring onion whites
½ cup thinly sliced french beans
2 tsp soya sauce

3 tbsp oil
Salt to taste

For the garnish
½ cup chopped spring onion greens

1. Heat the oil in a wok over a high flame, add the garlic and dry red chillies and stir-fry for a few seconds.
2. Add the cabbage, capsicum, spring onion whites and french beans and stir-fry over a high flame for 3-4 minutes.
3. Add the noodles, soya sauce and salt, mix well and stir-fry for a few minutes. Serve hot garnished with the spring onion greens.

Pan Fried Hakka Noodles

A meal by itself, this evergreen combination of mushrooms and green peas, prepared the Chinese way and served on a bed of crispy pan fried noodles, makes a perfect main course.

Preparation time: 10 minutes. Cooking time: 20 minutes. Serves 4.

For the noodles
3 cups boiled hakka noodles, page 99
3 tbsp oil

For the vegetables
2 cups sliced mushrooms
1 cup parboiled green peas
1 tbsp finely chopped garlic
1 to 2 green chillies, finely chopped
3 to 4 tsp soya sauce
1 heaped tbsp cornflour dissolved in ½ cup water
A pinch MSG (Mono Sodium Glutamate), optional

2 tbsps oil
Salt to taste

For the vegetables

1. Heat the oil in a wok over a high flame, add the garlic and green chillies and fry for a few seconds.
2. Add the mushrooms and green peas and sauté for a few minutes.
3. Add the soya sauce, cornflour mixture, MSG and salt and cook till the sauce thickens. Keep aside.

For the noodles

1. Heat the oil in a large frying pan.
2. Spread the noodles and cook over a slow flame until the noodles are lightly browned at the bottom. Turn them over and cook the other side until the noodles are lightly browned.

How to proceed

Transfer the noodles onto a serving plate and top with the vegetables.
Serve immediately.

Chinese Bhel

Pep yourself up with this famous Indo-Chinese dish. It's total fun food!

Preparation time: 10 minutes. No cooking. Serves 4.

4 cups crispy fried noodles, page 100
¼ cup finely chopped spring onions
2 tbsp finely chopped cabbage
2 tbsp finely chopped capsicum
2 tbsp deseeded and finely chopped tomatoes
2 tbsp finely chopped carrots

Sweet *khajur imli ki chutney* to taste
Schezuan sauce, page 91 to taste
Soya sauce to taste
Salt to taste

1. Mix the noodles, spring onions, cabbage, capsicum, tomatoes and carrots in a large bowl.
2. Add the chutney, both the sauces and salt according to taste.
   Toss well and serve immediately.

Vegetable Chow Mein

Chow mein is a style of preparation where the noodles are prepared separately and then topped with a choice of ingredients, according to your taste. Here we have used carrots, baby corn and mushrooms.

Preparation time: 15 minutes. Cooking time: 20 minutes. Serves 4.

For the noodles
3 cups boiled hakka noodles, page 99
1 tbsp hoisin sauce

For the vegetables
1 cup sliced onions
2 tsp grated ginger
2 tsp chopped garlic
2 tsp chopped celery
½ cup carrots, cut into thin strips
½ cup baby corn, cut into 4 (lengthwise)
2 cups sliced mushrooms
½ cup bean sprouts
1 tbsp oil
Salt to taste

To be mixed together into a sauce
½ cup hoisin sauce
2 tbsp cornflour
1 cup water

Other ingredients
1 tsp sesame (til) oil

For the noodles
Mix together the hoisin sauce and the noodles. Keep aside.

For the vegetables
1. Heat the oil in a wok over a high flame and sauté the onions, ginger, garlic and celery for a few seconds.
2. Add the carrots, baby corn, mushrooms and salt and sauté for 2 to 3 minutes till the vegetables soften.
3. Add the bean sprouts and the prepared sauce and bring to a boil. Keep aside.

How to proceed
1. In a non-stick pan (150 mm. (6") in diameter), heat the sesame oil and add the noodles. Arrange evenly on the surface of the pan to make a pancake.
   Cook till the noodles are golden brown in colour and lightly crisp.
2. Carefully turn the noodles around and cook over a slow flame for 3 to 4 minutes and then slide them on a serving plate.
   Serve immediately topped with the vegetables.

Handy tip: Use a mixture of soya sauce, tomato ketchup and chilli sauce in equal proportions if you do not have hoisin sauce.

Chinese Barbequed Tofu with Sesame Noodles

Delicately flavoured tofu cooked to perfection adds an unbeatable flavour to this noodle preparation.

Preparation time: 10 minutes. Cooking time: 10 minutes. Serves 4.

3 cups boiled flat noodles, page 99
1 cup cubed tofu (soya *paneer*)
2 tsp sesame *(til)* seeds
1 cup carrot, cut into thin strips
1 cup sliced spring onions
2 tbsp soya sauce
2 tbsp sugar
2 tbsp sesame (*til*) oil
Salt to taste

To be mixed into a marinade
2 tbsp soya sauce
2 tbsp hoisin sauce, page 14
2 tbsp vegetarian oyster sauce, page 16
1 tbsp finely chopped garlic
½ tsp Chinese 5 spice powder, page 14
1 tsp sugar
½ tsp dry red chilli flakes
Salt to taste

1. Marinate the tofu in the marinade for about one hour. Drain out the marinade and keep aside.

2. Heat the little oil on a non-stick pan and sauté the tofu cubes till they become golden brown. Drain on absorbent paper and keep aside.
3. Heat the remaining oil in a wok over high flame, add the sesame seeds, carrots and spring onions and sauté till the carrots are almost done.
4. Add the tofu, leftover marinade, soya sauce, sugar, boiled noodles and salt and mix well.
5. Heat for some time and serve immediately.

Stewed Noodles

This colourful and simple concoction of vegetables is a visual and culinary treat!

Preparation time: 10 minutes. Cooking time: 15 minutes. Serves 4.

3 cups boiled hakka noodles, page 99
½ cup green melon, cut into cubes
½ cup coloured capsicum (yellow, green, red) cubes
¼ cup dry shitake mushrooms, optional
½ cup blanched broccoli florets
4 nos. baby corn, sliced and blanched
2 cups clear vegetable stock, page 97
2 tbsp cornflour
2 tbsp soya sauce
Salt and pepper to taste

1. Soak the shitake mushrooms in lukewarm water for about 15 minutes.
2. Drain and discard the water. Keep aside.

3. Heat the oil in a wok over a high flame, add the vegetables and sauté for a few minutes.
4. Mix corn flour with the stock and add the mixture to the wok.
5. Stir in soya sauce, salt and pepper.
6. Adjust the water consistency to make a thin sauce.
7. Cook all the vegetable in the sauce for 5 minutes.
8. Add the noodles and bring to a boil.
   Serve immediately.

Schezuan Noodles

Picture on page 55.

"Schezuan" means spice. True to its name, this dish is a delectable blend of spicy flavours that are sure to tease your palate.

Preparation time: 15 minutes. Cooking time: 10 minutes. Serves 4.

4 cups boiled hakka noodles, page 99
2 tsp chopped garlic
1 tbsp chopped celery
2 cups finely sliced mixed vegetables (carrots, capsicum, cabbage, french beans)
¼ cup Schezuan sauce, page 91
½ cup bean sprouts
½ cup tofu (soya *paneer*) cubes
3 tbsp oil
1 tbsp chilli oil, page 102
Salt to taste

1. Heat the oil and chilli oil in a wok on a high flame, add the garlic and sauté till it turns golden brown in colour.

2. Add the celery and vegetables and sauté for 4 to 5 minutes.
3. Add the Schezuan sauce and cook for another minute.
4. Add the noodles, bean sprouts, tofu and salt and mix well. Toss for a few seconds and serve hot.

SCHEZUAN NOODLES : Recipe on page 53. →

Malaysian Noodles

An aesthetic presentation of soft noodles and bean curd combined with fresh vegetables and crunchy peanuts.

Preparation time: 10 minutes. Cooking time: 10 minutes. Serves 4.

3 cups boiled flat noodles, page 99
1 cup tofu (soya *paneer*) cubes
1 crushed garlic
4 spring onions chopped
½ cup carrot strips
½ cup thinly sliced capsicum
1 cup bean sprouts
2 tbsp roasted and chopped peanuts
¾ tsp chilli powder
2 tsp sugar
2 tbsp soya sauce
1 tbsp lemon juice
4 tbsp oil

Salt to taste

Other ingredients
Oil for deep-frying

1. Heat the oil in a wok over a high flame and fry the tofu in it till golden brown.
2. Drain on absorbent paper and keep aside.
3. Heat the oil in another wok over a high flame and add the crushed garlic.
4. Add the fried tofu, spring onions, carrots, capsicum, bean sprouts, peanuts and noodles.
5. Add the chilli powder, sugar, soya sauce, lemon juice and salt and toss well. Serve hot.

Singapore Rice Noodles

Translucent, pretty looking rice noodles, aesthetically flavoured with Asian flavourings like cumin and coriander, these noodles will melt in your mouth and please every culinary sense.

Preparation time: 10 minutes. Cooking time: 10 minutes. Serves 4.

To be mixed together

3 cups cooked rice noodles, refer handy tip
½ cup bean sprouts
1 cup chopped spring onion greens
¼ tsp coriander (dhania) powder
a pinch of turmeric powder (haldi)
1 tbsp sesame (*til*) oil
Salt to taste

Other ingredients

½ cup sliced spring onion whites
1 tsp chopped garlic

¼ cup carrots, cut into thin strips
¼ cup french beans, cut into thin strips
¼ cup shredded red cabbage, optional
¼ cup sliced red capsicum
¼ cup sliced capsicum
1 tsp oil
Salt to taste

1. Heat the oil in a wok on a high flame, add the spring onion whites and garlic and sauté for a few seconds.
2. Add the carrots, french beans, red cabbage, red capsicum, capsicum and salt and sauté for some time till the vegetables soften. Sprinkle some water if required.
3. Add the rice noodles mixture and toss well over a high flame.
4. Spoon out into a serving plate and serve immediately.

Handy tip: To cook rice noodles, soak them in boiling hot water for 10 to 15 minutes or as the instruction on the package specify. Drain the water and again dip into cold water in order to arrest any further cooking. Drain and use as required.

VARIATION : SINGAPORE RICE

Use steamed rice instead of rice noodles in the above recipe.

American Chopsuey

Picture on page 2.

A delightful preparation of crispy noodles served with stir-fried vegetables and a tangy sauce. Interestingly, a literal translation of this recipe means 'savoury mess'!

Preparation time: 30 minutes.   Cooking time: 10 minutes.   Serves 4.

1 cup boiled hakka noodles, page 99
1½ cups crispy fried noodles, page 100
2 cups shredded cabbage
½ cup sliced onions
½ cup bean sprouts
½ cup parboiled french beans, cut diagonally into thin strips
½ cup sliced and parboiled carrots
½ tsp MSG (Mono Sodium Glutamate), optional
1 tsp chilli sauce
4 tsp oil
Salt to taste

For the tangy sauce
¼ cup brown vinegar

¼ cup sugar
1 cup water
2 tbsp *maida* (plain flour)
1 tbsp soya sauce
4 tbsp tomato ketchup

To serve
8 steamed vegetable wontons, page 22

For the tangy sauce
Combine all the ingredients for the sauce in a pan, mix well and bring to a boil. Cook until the sauce thickens. Keep aside.

How to proceed
1. Heat the oil in another wok over a high flame and add the cabbage, onions, bean sprouts, french beans, carrots and MSG. Stir-fry for 3 to 4 minutes.
2. Add half the tangy sauce, boiled noodles, chilli sauce and salt and cook for a few minutes.
3. Add half of the fried noodles and mix well.
   Serve hot, topped with the remaining fried noodles, steamed vegetable wontons and the remaining tangy sauce.

Rice

Vegetable Fried Rice

Picture on cover.

This is an indispensable part of Chinese meals. To keep the rice grains separate, spread the cooked rice grains on a tray and allow it to cool. Rub a little oil on the cooked rice and keep aside till you require it.

Preparation time: 15 minutes. Cooking time: 30 minutes. Serves 4.

3 cups Chinese rice, page 98
½ cup french beans, cut diagonally into thin strips
½ cup carrots, cut into long thin strips
½ cup capsicum, cut into long thin strips
¼ cup bean sprouts
¼ cup sliced mushrooms
1 tbsp chopped celery
1 cup chopped spring onion whites

1 tsp soya sauce
1 cup chopped spring onion greens
A pinch MSG (Mono Sodium Glutamate), optional
1 tbsp oil
Salt to taste

1. Heat the oil in a wok over a high flame, add the french beans, carrots, capsicum, bean sprouts, mushrooms, celery, spring onion whites and MSG and sauté for 3 to 4 minutes till the vegetables soften.
2. Add the rice, soya sauce, spring onion greens and salt. Mix well and sauté for 2 minutes.
   Serve hot.

VARIATION: MUSHROOM RICE

Add soaked shitake mushrooms, oyster mushrooms and button mushrooms instead of french beans, carrots and capsicum in the above recipe.

BURNT GARLIC RICE

Deep fry ½ cup of chopped garlic till golden brown and add it in the above recipe.

Stewed Rice

Picture on facing page.

Chinese rice stewed with subtly flavoured vegetables.

Preparation time: 15 minutes. Cooking time: 10 minutes. Serves 4.

3 cups Chinese rice, page 98
1 cup blanched cauliflower florets
8 to 10 baby corn, sliced thinly
1 cup sliced capsicum
1 cup parboiled and sliced carrots
1 cup chopped spring onions
1 cup diagonally sliced cucumber
¼ tsp MSG (Mono Sodium Glutamate)
½ cup milk
1 cup clear vegetable stock, page 97
1 level tbsp cornflour dissolved in 2 tbsp water
½ tsp sugar
2 tbsp oil
Salt to taste

1. Heat the oil in a wok over a high flame, add the cauliflower, baby corn, capsicum, carrots, spring onions, cucumber and MSG and stir-fry for 3-4 minutes.
2. Add the milk, stock and cornflour mixture and cook till the mixture thickens.
3. Add the rice, sugar and salt and mix well. Cook for a few minutes.
   Serve hot.

STEWED RICE : Recipe above. →

Triple Schezuan Rice

If you cannot make up your mind whether to have rice or noodles, just have this.

Preparation time: 15 minutes. Cooking time: 10 minutes. Serves 4.

2 cups Chinese rice, page 98
1 cup chopped boiled hakka noodles, page 99
1 tsp chopped garlic
2 tsp chopped celery
1 cup finely sliced vegetables (carrots, capsicum, cabbage)
2 to 3 drops orange-red colour
2 tbsp oil
Salt to taste
½ cp Schezuan sauce, page 91

1. Heat the oil in a wok over a high flame, add the garlic and sauté till it turns golden in colour.
2. Add the celery and vegetables and sauté for 2 to 3 minutes.
3. Add the Schezuan sauce and cook for another minute.
4. Add the rice, noodles, orange-red colour and salt and mix well.
5. Toss for a few seconds till all the ingredients are mixed. Serve hot.

5 Spice Tofu and Bean Sprouts Rice

The delicate blend of flavours and textures in this dish may not appeal to all, but it is a must for those who like to experiment beyond the traditional Chinese fried rice.

Preparation time: 15 minutes. Cooking time: 10 minutes. Serves 4.

3 cups Chinese rice, page 98
1 cup fried tofu (soya *paneer*)
1½ tsp Chinese 5 spice powder, page 14
½ cup bean sprouts
1 cup sliced spring onions
a pinch sugar
2 tbsp oil
Salt to taste

1. Heat the oil in a wok over a high flame, add the spring onions and sauté till they are tender.
2. Add the Chinese 5 spice powder and sauté for ½ a minute.
3. Add the bean sprouts and tofu and mix well.
4. Add the rice, sugar and salt and toss well. Serve hot.

Vegetable Dishes

Vegetable Manchurian

When you eat these deep fried vegetable balls in a soya-based sauce, do not let mundane things like the weighing scale bother you! Just dig into these deep-fried delights and enjoy every bite!

Preparation time: 15 minutes. Cooking time: 20 minutes. Serves 4.

For the vegetable balls
2 cups finely chopped cabbage
¼ cup grated carrots
? cup chopped spring onions
2 tbsp cornflour
2 tbsp plain flour (*maida*)
2 tsp finely chopped garlic
1 tsp finely chopped green chilli
¼ tsp MSG (Mono Sodium Glutamate), optional
Salt and pepper to taste
Oil for deep-frying

For the sauce
2 tsp finely chopped garlic
2 tsp finely chopped green chillies
1 tsp finely chopped ginger

1 cup clear vegetable stock, page 97 or water
1 tbsp soya sauce
2 tbsp cornflour dissolved in 1 cup of water
2 pinches sugar
2 tbsp oil
Salt to taste

For the vegetable balls

1. Mix together all the ingredients and shape the mixture into small balls. If you find it difficult to form balls, sprinkle a little water to bind the mixture.
2. Deep-fry in hot oil until golden brown. Drain on absorbent paper and keep aside.

For the sauce

1. Heat the oil in a wok over a high flame. Add the garlic, green chillies and ginger and stir-fry for a few seconds.
2. Add the stock, soya sauce, cornflour mixture, sugar and salt and simmer for a few minutes.

How to serve

Just before serving, put the vegetable balls in the sauce and bring to a boil. Serve hot.

Chilli Potatoes

This versatile dish can be served as a starter or as an accompaniment to the main meal.

Preparation time: 10 minutes. Cooking time: 10 minutes. Serves 4.

4 large potatoes (80% cooked)
1 tsp finely chopped garlic
½ tsp finely chopped ginger
1 tsp chopped green chillies
1 tsp tomato ketchup
2 tbsp soya sauce
½ tsp chilli sauce
2 tsp cornflour
4 tbsp oil
Salt to taste

For the garnish
sliced spring onions

1. Peel and cut the cooked potatoes into fingers.
2. Heat the oil in a wok over a high flame, add the potato fingers and cook for a few

minutes till they turn golden brown. Drain on an absorbent paper and keep aside.

3. In the same oil, add the garlic, ginger and green chillies and stir-fry for a few seconds. Add the potato fingers, tomato ketchup, soya sauce, chilli sauce and salt.
4. Mix the cornflour in ½ cup of water. Add to the mixture and cook for 1 to 2 minutes.

Serve hot topped with spring onions.

VARIATION : CHILLI PANEER

Use fried paneer strips instead of potatoes.

Sweet and Sour Vegetables

This easy to make, popular vegetable dish and Chinese Fried Rice are made for each other.

Preparation time: 20 minutes. Cooking time: 10 minutes. Serves 6 to 8.

¼ cup parboiled cauliflower florets
¼ cup parboiled and diagonally cut french beans
¼ cup parboiled carrots cubes
¼ cup cabbage cubes
¼ cup cucumber cubes
¼ cup capsicum cubes
¼ cup chopped onions
4 sticks celery, chopped
½ tsp MSG (Mono Sodium Glutamate), optional
4 tbsp oil
Salt to taste

For the sauce
¾ cup brown vinegar
¾ cup sugar
1 cup water
2 tbsp cornfour
2 tbsp soya sauce
¼ cup tomato ketchup

To serve
Chillies in vinegar, page 90
Chilli sauce

For the sauce
Place all the ingredients for the sauce in a vessel, mix well and put to boil. Go on cooking and stirring until the sauce thickens.

How to proceed
1. Heat the oil thoroughly in a wok over a high flame and add the french beans, carrots, cabbage, cucumber, capsicum, onions and celery and MSG.
2. Stir-fry over a high flame for 3 to 4 minutes.
3. Add the prepared sauce and salt and heat for 2 minutes.
   Serve hot with green chillies in vinegar and chilli sauce.

Handy tip : You can add a few pieces of chopped pineapple at step 2 to make this dish even more tangy.

Vegetable Hongkong Style

Picture on facing page.

A variety of spices and sauces come together to make this delectable veggie preparation. Goes well with Fried Rice.

Preparation time: 10 minutes. Cooking time: 5 minutes. Serves 4.

2 cups parboiled mixed vegetable cubes (carrots, french beans, baby corn)
1 capsicum, cut into big pieces
2 tsp finely chopped ginger
1 tsp finley chopped garlic
3 to 4 whole dry red chillies, broken into pieces
2 pinches MSG (Mono Sodium Glutamate), optional
2 tbsp soya sauce
2 tsp white vinegar
2 tsp chilli sauce
1½ cups clear vegetable stock, page 97, or water

VEGETABLE HONGKONG STYLE : Recipe above. →

2 tbsp cornflour, dissolved in ¼ cup water
A pinch sugar
2 tbsp oil
Salt and pepper to taste

1. Heat the oil in a wok over a high flame, add the vegetables, capsicum, ginger, garlic, dry red chillies and MSG and stir-fry for 2 minutes.
2. Add the soya sauce, vinegar, chilli sauce, sugar, salt and pepper and mix well.
3. Add the cornflour mixture and stock and simmer for some time.
   Serve hot.

5 Treasure Vegetables

Colourful, simple and tasty you can use any five vegetables of your choice for this dish.

Preparation time: 15 minutes. Cooking time: 25 minutes. Serves 4.

½ cup baby corn, cut into 2 vertically
¼ cup fresh mushrooms, quartered
½ cup carrots, cut into thin strips
½ cup broccoli florets
¼ cup chopped onions
1½ tsp finely chopped garlic
½ cup bean sprouts
½ cup fried tofu (soya *paneer*) cubes
1½ tsp oil
Salt to taste

To be mixed into a sauce
½ tsp soya sauce
½ tsp sesame (til) oil
¼ cup water
1½ tsp cornflour
1 tsp hoisin sauce, page 14

1. Parboil the baby corn, mushrooms, carrots and broccoli till they are tender.
2. Drain and immerse them in cold water. Drain again and keep aside.
3. Heat the oil in another pan and add the onions and garlic and sauté for 1 to 2 minutes.
4. Add the bean sprouts and fried tofu and sauté for another minute.
5. Add the parboiled vegetables and salt and stir-fry over a high flame for a few minutes.
6. Add the sauce mixture and bring to a boil, stirring continuously.
   Serve immediately.

Vegetables in Mala Sauce

All it takes is a few minutes of sautéing and cooking in the wok to make this exotic preparation!

Preparation time: 10 minutes. Cooking time: 5 minutes. Serves 4.

½ cup broccoli florets
½ cup asparagus, cut into 1″pieces
½ cup sliced baby corn
½ cup soaked chinese mushrooms *(shitake)*, optional
8 cleaned water chestnuts *(singoda)*
1 tbsp grated garlic
1 tbsp red chilli paste
½ cup chopped spring onions
3 tbsp soya sauce
1 tsp Chinese 5 spice powder, page 14

2 tsp sugar
2 tbsp cornflour dissolved in ¼ cup water
2 tbsp oil
Salt as per taste

1. Heat the oil in a wok over a high flame, add the garlic and red chilli paste.
2. Add all the remaining ingredients and sauté for some time.
3. Add ½ cup of water and cook stirring continuously till the mixture thickens. Serve hot.

Tri Mushrooms in Lemon Sauce

The fantastic combination of lemon and coriander sauce with mushrooms makes this recipe irresistible!

Preparation time: 10 minutes. Cooking time: 10 minutes. Serves 4.

½ cup thickly sliced mushrooms
½ cup shitake mushrooms
½ cup sliced oyster mushrooms
2 tbsp chopped coriander
1 tsp grated lemon rind
1 tsp oil
Salt to taste

For the Chinese white sauce
¼ cup finely chopped onions
1 tsp chopped ginger
1 tsp chopped garlic
¼ cup white wine

2 tbsp cornflour dissolved in 3 cups of clear vegetable stock, page 97
A pinch of sugar
½ tbsp oil
Salt to taste

For the Chinese white sauce

1. Heat the oil in a pan, add the onions, ginger and garlic and sauté till the onions are translucent.
2. Add the wine and cook on a high flame for a few seconds.
3. Add the cornflour mixture and cook till the sauce thickens.
4. Add sugar and salt, mix well and use as required.

How to proceed

1. Soak the shitake mushrooms in lukewarm water. Drain out the water and keep the mushrooms aside.
2. Heat the oil in a pan, add all varieties of mushrooms and salt and sauté for a few seconds over a high flame.
3. Add the Chinese white sauce, coriander and salt and cook for some more time.
4. Add some water, if required, to adjust consistency.
5. Take the pan off the heat, add the lemon rind and serve immediately.

Hot Garlic Sauce with Baby Corn and Broccoli

Picture on page 85.

A popular choice, this combination of baby corn and broccoli tastes as good as it sounds.

Preparation time: 10 minutes. Cooking time: 10 minutes. Serves 4.

1 cup sliced baby corn
1 cup parboiled broccoli florets
2 tsp finely chopped ginger
2 tsp finely chopped garlic
2 tsp finely chopped green chillies
A pinch MSG (Mono Sodium Glutamate), optional
½ cup tomato purée
2 tsp cornflour dissolved in ½ cup of water
A pinch of sugar, optional
2 tbsp oil
Salt to taste

1. Heat the oil in a wok over a high flame, add the ginger, garlic and green chillies and stir-fry for a few seconds.
2. Add the baby corn and broccoli and MSG and cook for a few minutes.
3. Add the tomato purée and mix well.
4. Add the cornflour mixture and salt and cook for a few minutes. If you like, add a pinch of sugar.

   Serve hot.

HOT GARLIC SAUCE WITH BABY CORN AND BROCCOLI: Recipe on page 83. →

Saiwoo Vegetables

Strips of batter-coated and deep-fried vegetables are enveloped in an unusual sauce, made absolutely irresistible by the interplay of honey, five spice powder and dry red chillies.

Preparation time: 20 minutes. Cooking time: 15 minutes. Serves 4.

For crispy vegetables

2 cups parboiled mixed vegetables, (carrots, baby corn, capscium), cut into thick cubes
5 tbsp cornflour dissolved in ½ cup water
Salt to taste
Oil for deep-frying

For the honey 5-spice sauce

2 tbsp honey
2 tsp soya sauce
A pinch MSG (Mono Sodium Glutamate), optional
½ tsp Chinese 5 spice powder, page 14
2 tsp sugar
Salt to taste

Other ingredients

½ cup chopped spring onion whites
2 tbsp chopped ginger
2 tsp chopped garlic
4 whole dry red chillies, broken into pieces
2 sliced green chillies
2 tbsp Schezuan sauce, page 91
2 tbsp oil
Salt to taste

For serving
½ cup spring onion greens

For the crispy vegetables
1. Add the salt and vegetables to the cornflour mixture.
2. Mix lightly so that the batter coats the vegetables.
3. Deep-fry the vegetables in hot oil until crisp. Remove, drain on absorbent paper and keep aside.

For the honey 5-spice sauce
1. Heat the honey over a low flame.
2. Add the soya sauce, MSG, Chinese 5 spice powder, sugar and salt and mix well. Mix well and keep aside.

How to proceed
1. Heat 2 tablespoons of oil in a wok over a high flame and add the spring onion whites, ginger and garlic and sauté for a few seconds.
2. Add the dry red chillies and green chillies and sauté till the red chillies turn brown.
3. Add the Schezuan sauce, the honey-5 spice sauce and salt and cook for a few seconds.
4. Toss in the crispy fried vegetables and spring onion greens and serve immediately.

Handy tip : Do not cook for a long time after adding the vegetables as the vegetables will get soggy.

Accompanients

Khimchi

This crunchy sweet and spicy preparation is the first dish that arrives when you dine at a Chinese restaurant. Khimchi generally refers to any preserved vegetables, and are usually eaten in the winter when fresh vegetables are scarce.

In this recipe, you can also use cucumber and carrot strips along with cabbage. Just remember to adjust the other ingredients proportionately.

Preparation time: 5 minutes. No cooking. Makes 1 cup.

1 cup cabbage, cut into 25 mm. (1") cubes
1 tsp chilli powder
1 tbsp powdered sugar
1 tbsp white vinegar
1 tsp salt

1. Combine all the ingredients in a bowl and mix well.
2. Keep aside for at least an hour before serving.

Handy tip : When stored in an air-tight container this can be refrigerated for a few days.

Chillies in Vinegar

Chillies add extra punch to the vinegar that's often served with Chinese food. I often make some and store in a large bottle.

Preparation time: a few minutes. No Cooking. Makes 1 cup.

6 to 7 green chillies, chopped
1 cup white vinegar

Add the green chillies to the vinegar. Store in an air-tight container.
Use as required.

VARIATION : Green chillies can be substituted with fresh red chillies to get red chillies in vinegar.

Schezuan Sauce

This fiery sauce in one of my favourites! Chinese cooking can never be complete without this fantastic blend of hot spices and condiments.

Preparation time: 10 minutes. Cooking time: 5 minutes. Makes 1 cup.

For the paste
20 whole dry red chillies
¼ cup chopped garlic

Other ingredients
1 tbsp finely chopped garlic
1 tsp finely chopped green chillies
½ tbsp grated ginger
2 tbsp finely chopped onions
1 tsp finely chopped celery
1 cup clear vegetable stock, page 97
1 tbsp cornflour dissolved in 2 tbsp water
1 tbsp white vinegar

2 tsp sugar
a pinch MSG (Mono Sodium Glutamate), optional
3 tbsp oil
Salt to taste

For the paste

1. Boil 1 cup of water.
2. Add the dry red chillies and garlic and cook for 8 to 10 minutes. Cool.
3. Drain out the water. Grind into a smooth paste in a blender using a little water.

How to proceed

1. Heat the oil in a wok over a high flame and sauté the garlic, green chillies, ginger, onions and celery for 1 minute.
2. Add the paste and sauté again for 1 minute.
3. Add the vegetable stock and mix well. Add the cornflour mixture, vinegar, sugar, MSG and salt. Bring to a boil and keep aside.
   Use as required.

Chilli Garlic Sauce

This tongue tingling combination can serve as both cooking and table sauce.

Preparation time: 10 minutes. No cooking. Makes 1 cup.

¾ cup finely minced tomatoes
½ tbsp grated garlic
½ tsp chopped green chillies
1 tbsp chopped coriander
1 tbsp tomato ketchup
1 tsp white vinegar
¼ tsp powdered sugar
1 tsp chilli oil
A pinch MSG (Mono Sodium Glutamate), optional
Salt to taste

Mix all the ingredients and blend in a blender to a smooth sauce.
Use as required.

Red Garlic Sauce

No Chinese kitchen can ever be complete without this. An absolute must when serving Chinese food!

Preparation time: 5 minutes. Cooking time: a few minutes. Makes 1½ cups.

1 tbsp finely chopped garlic
½ tsp finely chopped green chillies
1 tbsp finely chopped spring onions
1 tbsp finely chopped onions
1 tbsp tomato ketchup
¾ cup clear vegetable stock, page 97
1 tbsp cornflour dissolved in 2 tbsp of water
A pinch MSG (Mono Sodium Glutamate), optional
2 tbsp oil
Salt to taste

1. Heat the oil in a wok over a high flame and fry the garlic, green chillies, spring onions and onions for 1 minute.

2. Add the tomato ketchup, vegetable stock and cornflour mixture. Mix well and cook for 1 minute.
3. Add the MSG and salt. Mix well.
   Use as required.

Green Garlic Sauce

This refreshing mix of flavours awakens the taste buds.

Preparation time: 5 minutes. No cooking. Makes ½ cup.

1 tbsp finely chopped coriander
1 tsp finely chopped green chillies
2 tbsp finely chopped fresh green garlic
Juice of 1 lemon
1 tbsp powdered sugar
2 tsp white vinegar
Salt to taste

1. Mix all the ingredients together in a bowl.
2. Adjust the sweetness as required. Store refrigerated in an air-tight container. Use as required.

Handy tip: If fresh green garlic is not available use 1 tbsp of finely chopped garlic instead and add 1 more tbsp of chopped coriander.

Basic Recipes

Clear Vegetable Stock

The absence of spices differentiates Chinese stock from the French version. While a recipe for French stock might call for a pinch of thyme or a few garlic cloves, the Chinese believe that spicing masks the flavour of the stock. Seasonings are added later, depending on the requirements of individual recipes. This stock is used for soups and gravies to add flavour and body to them.

Preparation time: 5 minutes. Cooking time: 20 minutes. Makes 4½ cups.

½ cup roughly chopped cabbage
½ cup roughly chopped carrots
¼ cup chopped celery
2 tbsp chopped spring onions
3 to 4 cauliflower florets

1. Boil all the vegetables in 6 cups of water on a medium flame for 15 to 20 minutes, till it reduces to about 4½ cups.
2. Allow the vegetables to settle at the bottom of the vessel and drain out the stock. Discard the vegetables. Use as required.

Chinese Rice

The Chinese have developed rice-making into an art. Perfect fried rice requires that each grain of rice is separate. Here's how to make rice the Chinese way…

Preparation time: 5 minutes. Cooking time: 15 minutes. Makes 2 cups.

1 cup long grained rice
2 tbsp oil
1 tsp salt

1. Wash the rice thoroughly and soak in 3 cups of water for 30 minutes. Drain and keep aside.
2. Boil 6 to 8 cups water, add salt and 1 tbsp of oil.
3. Add the rice to the boiling water. Cook till the rice is 85% cooked.
4. Pour into a colander and let the water drain out. Pour some cold water on the rice to arrest further cooking.
5. Let all the water from the rice drain out and ensure that the rice does not contain any moisture.
6. Add the remaining 1 tbsp of oil and toss the rice in it
7. Spread the cooked rice on a flat surface till it is cool. Use as required.

Boiled Noodles

The Chinese believe that every meal should contain an equal proportion of starch and vegetables. Noodles comprise one starch group that they rely on to provide this harmonious dietary balance.

Here a simple technique to cook the noodles to perfection...

Preparation time: 5 minutes. Cooking time: 10 minutes. Makes 4 cups.

½ packet (100 grams) hakka noodles/flat noodles
2 tbsp oil
Salt to taste

1. Boil water and add 1 tbsp oil and salt.
2. Add the noodles and allow the water to come to a boil, then simmer till the noodles are cooked.
3. Remove from the fire and drain out all the water.
4. Pour some cold water on the noodles to arrest further cooking.
5. Let all the water drain out and ensure that the noodles do not contain any moisture.
6. Add the remaining 1 tbsp of oil and mix lightly. This will prevent the noodles from sticking together. Use as required.

Handy tip: When the noodles are cooked they will rise to the top and also change colour.

Crispy Fried Noodles

Parboiled and deep-fried noodles make a great topping for soups, and also form the principal ingredient for Chopsuey. I enjoy these drizzled with Schezuan sauce at the beginning of my Chinese meal.

Preparation time: 5 minutes. Cooking time: 20 minutes. Serves 4.

1 packet (200 grams) Chinese noodles
2 tbsp oil
salt to taste
Oil for deep frying

1. Boil 4 cups of water and add 2 tbsp of oil. Add the noodles while stirring occasionally and cook until they are parboiled. Drain well.
2. Spread the noodles on a clean piece of cloth and allow to dry for at least 2 to 3 hours.

3. Heat the oil in a wok or frying pan over a medium flame. Fry small quantities of noodles at a time in the hot oil until golden brown.
4. Remove the noodles from the oil and drain on absorbent paper. Repeat with the remaining noodles.
   Use as required.

Handy tip : If the noodles still look a bit soft after drying, sprinkle a little cornflour over them and then deep fry them.

Crispy Rice

Adds crunch to any recipe!

Preparation time: 5 minutes. Cooking time: 20 minutes. Makes 1½ cups.

¾ cup long grained rice

1. Boil plenty of water in a pan. Add the rice and cook.
2. When the rice is 90% cooked, drain out all the water.

3. Spread the rice on a large tray, cover with a piece of cloth and sun-dry until crisp.
4. Store in an air-tight container.
5. When required, place the dried rice in a strainer and deep-fry for a few seconds till the rice puffs up. Drain on absorbent paper. Use immediately.

Note : The dried rice lasts for 3 to 4 months on the kitchen shelf if stored in an air-tight container.

Chilli Oil

The warm pungent aroma of this chilli-charged oil adds zing to our cooking.

Preparation time: 5 minutes. Cooking time: 5 minutes. Makes 1 cup.

15 to 20 whole dry red chillies, broken into pieces
1 cup oil

1. Heat the oil to smoking point and add the chillies and switch off the gas.
2. Cover and keep aside for 2 hours. Strain and store the oil in a bottle, discarding the chillies. Use as required.

Mini Series by *Tarla Dalal*

Healthy Breakfast

Healthy Snacks

Healthy Soups & Salads

Healthy Juices

Fast Foods Made Healthy

Calcium Rich Recipes

Iron Rich Recipes

Forever Young Diet

Home Remedies

Low Cholesterol Recipes